THE SECRET LIFE OF A SIX FIGURE ENTREPRENEUR

INSIGHTS INTO A BUSINESS OWNERS LIFESTYLE

Bonus! - As a way of saying thanks, here's a short book that is guaranteed to excel your business career. It helped me greatly and will do the same for you if you can internalise the concepts.

Download Here → *http://goo.gl/iYx5aC*

THE SECRET LIFE OF A SIX FIGURE ENTREPRENEUR

Insights into a Business Owners LifeStyle

Written By:

Mateen S

Brought to you by AffEngineer.com

www.AffEngineer.com Copyright © 2015 by AffEngineer Publishing

Disclaimer

Table of Contents

Introduction

Three years ago I made the biggest, most important decision of my life.

With little to no business plan, I decided to quit work and try my luck at entrepreneurship. Was it worth it? Many had doubted my decision at the start. Even I thought I was being a little rash. Now, Three years and 100s of thousands of dollars later, I couldn't have been more confident in that decision.

It took a lot of pain staking hours to get here though. A lot of frustrating business plans that fell through. Money spent on books, course, marketing that made me $0.

The whole ideal has forced me to change and I'm no more the person I was Three years ago. This book is about my mindset now and what an average day into my business looks like. I wondered about this a lot when I first started. 'What would a day in the life of Mark Zuckerberg or Bill Gates or Steve Jobs look like'? I'm no Mark, Bill or Steve but I've found a process that makes me money and I know what I need to do to maintain that business.

What is an Entrepreneur?

First let's try and understand what an entrepreneur is. More importantly, who falls under this category.

It's an interesting title. One that can be self given or one that people start to refer to you as.

Without checking the dictionary, my simple definition of an entrepreneur is one that wants to make a monetary change to either their personal finances or the world as a whole. In layman's terms, they want to make money the non-traditional working way.

Some entrepreneurs are motivated by wanting to change how a certain part of the world works. They see a problem and dedicate their life to fix it. Some are motivated by the chance to have enough money and time to do what they desire.

Whether you're making money or not at this stage, it doesn't really matter. You can recognise entrepreneurship by the passion in someones eyes when they talk about a certain idea or concept.

I've known people who can talk for hours about an industry you have no clue about. They've been working at their business for years and although they may not be where they want to be, they have a strong entrepreneur spirit.

Major Differences

The more time you spend doing something, the more you learn about it. It's only natural. There are certain characteristics that begin to evolve into something else. Either you were born thinking a certain way or the entrepreneur life forced you to change and fixate your opinions accordingly. The below points are a few differences in how the average person may think about something compared to an entrepreneur. I've noticed a consistency in the type of thinking I share with many others so am confident much of it applies almost universally.

Note: - From here onwards, I'm going to refer to two types of people in this book. An *'Entrepreneur'* and the *'Average Person'*. Of course, every 'average person' is unique in their own way. My use of this term is only to refer to everyone that isn't an entrepreneur. A 'non-entrepreneur'.

Time vs Money

Your time is what you trade for money. It's something we don't really think about but our 8 hour work day shift is worth a set amount of dollars for a company which they compensate you for.

Average Person

The average person is happy to make this trade off for a set amount of money. This amount will increase depending on bonuses and the times of the year. You might get paid a little extra on weekends or night shifts but it's more or less fixed in concrete. There's only so much money you can make for that day, month, year but you're ok with that.

Entrepreneur

The Entrepreneur is not ok with this. They work hard some days but other days they don't do anything at all. How can they be paid the same amount?

The idea of limitless earning potential gets their heart racing.

There have been days I've made $0. There have been other days I've earned $1000s. Both days I've put a different amount of effort in. This is the life that makes more sense to me. I'm more in control of how much I earn.

Priorities

Average Person

Everyone has interests and hobbies. Things they'd much rather be doing instead of working. The average person is ok to sacrifice them all to earn money at a fixed rate. The thought of not being able to spend time doing what they love frustrates them but the fear or risk involved in doing what they love with a reduction in pay is more scary.

Entrepreneur

An entrepreneur can't let this happen. They were once working at a job and not doing what they loved frustrated them too. The only difference is that this frustration was greater than the fear of not being able to make it in entrepreneurship. They were willing to risk it all to make it work in the hopes that they could one day dedicate their life to do what they love.

Don't get me wrong, I'm not against people that work full-time. I'm not against anyone doing anything. The world is an open road to anyone and different people find satisfaction doing different things.

The order of priorities in your head can dictate the way you think about things. Your number one priority is predominantly going to be the one dictating most of your actions. Be wise on what you priorities. Is it financial security or freedom?

Productivity vs Smarts

Average Person
The average person has tonnes of ideas but doesn't do anything about it. They might have an idea list registry, plans, spreadsheets that auto-calculate how much they'd make if they had x customers after x amount of years.
They got good grades and feel they're smart. They are smart, in the eyes of everyone else but this is the biggest thing holding them back.

Entrepreneur
The entrepreneur might not be the brightest light in the street but he's a doer. He has no plans or idea lists but when he sees an opportunity he'll be the first to give it a shot in the slim chances he makes a fortune. Most of the times they fall through but his chance will eventually come.

Being smart isn't enough. You have to put things into effect to see what happens. The headstrong person who just puts half-baked plans into action to learn what the outcome might be will always win over someone who dwells on research, planing and other backend tasks too much. To the point where they never feel ready to put their plan in action and consequently don't.

You'll never learn what modifications you need to make to your business until you put it out there.

Conform vs Don't Care

Average Person

The average person has been conforming most of their life. It's hard for them to do things that get them weird looks from people. They don't like have no answers to things and fitting in is very important to them.

Entrepreneur

The entrepreneur doesn't care as much. If he needs to quit his job and live out of a caravan to make this work, he/she will. People will ask questions and yes, it is sad and frustrating to have no answer or an answer that's not impressive but it doesn't matter.

That's not important right now.

Entrepreneurship is a roller coaster. I'll take you real high and drop you to the ground. You have to be comfortable being in both places at any time. You have to be comfortable driving a beat up Camry till you can afford something better. You might even have to move in with your parents to cut costs.

At the end of the day you have to do what you

have to do. Caring about what other people think should be the last of your worries.

Risk over Safety

It's more important to be safe and secure than to be in a non-financially secure place but still content. The average person hates risk. Their body can't handle it. Some might work well under pressure but the thought of having no income is sickening.

Some are happy with their financial positions even though they know they deserve much better. This type of thinking plays into their relationships sometimes. They're stuck with their relationship even though they know it's toxic and deserve much better. To people like this, it's more important to believe they have it all then to actually have anything real.

Entrepreneurs

They see through it all. Risk is scary but not almost as scary as being stuck in the same work routine for years. Not nearly as scary as being on the death bed thinking back on all the opportunities they missed out on because they thought it was too risky.

They definitely care about being safe but the

'worst case scenario' doesn't seem too bad for them. They can deal with it. Down grading their car, moving in with their parents, cutting living costs. It's all part of the process to them.

Risk is something the begin to be comfortable with. They deal with it on a daily basis. Their whole livelihood is at stake with every decision they make. No one guarantees them a pay-check but they'll put in 100s of hours to see an idea through.

An Average Day

The daily activities of an entrepreneur are completely different to someone that works a full-time job.

Within the entrepreneurship circle, there's common activities that are understood as being good for your business. From healthy eating to exercise it's a full program of activities that work in sync with each other to create a healthy dose of productivity and motivation.

My average day is unique to me but is also similar to many others. Maybe the order of when I do things are different but at the end of the day the important things get done.

Below is my average working day.

5am

The alarm rings. I set it at 5am because I wanted to challenge myself to wake up early. The early hours of the day are the most serene. They're quit, most of the world is asleep. There's nothing new on FaceBook or Instagram or Snapchat. Distractions are a bare minimum and the more work you can do in the mornings, the better.

I'll reach to my phone, turn off the alarm and lie in bed for a while thinking of what I'm going to do. I might even reset the alarm to 5.30 but most of the times, I'll get up and get going.

5.30

The next half an hour is my morning routine. I'll have a nice big glass of water and wait a 5 to 10 minutes as the liquids go around waking up my body. I'll start to feel a slow but steady rush of being awake.

During that 5-10 minutes, I'll pull out a box of nut, apricot and date bites I made the a few days before.. They each have a healthy dose of carbs, fats and proteins and can be eaten while I'm working. I'll spend the half hour till 6 o' clock eating them and drinking more water. I hate feeling hungry while I work so I try and fill myself up with 500-800 calories of healthy raw food. Food that wakes me right up. Sometimes it's these bites, sometimes it's a raw banana/strawberry/avacado smoothie. Whatever the meal, it consists of something real healthy so I'm ready to go.

My mornings are the most important times of the day for me. In-fact, if I don't get my morning right, it'll most likely put me off for the rest of the day.

6am

Ok, work time has started. The next 4 hours are going to be a straight run of pure, uninterrupted and important work. Work that doesn't involve reading books or watching youtube tutorials.

This is work that is important. Think I don't always enjoy doing but need to get done.

Either they're making advertisements on FaceBook and running traffic to my sites or they're writing out 2-3,000 words for my eBook.

It could be working on a website I've been thinking of for a while or even writing blog posts for my blog. Again, a lot of this stuff is tedious and gets boring after a while but they're the core life of my business. Without a healthy dose of them everyday, my output and consequently my income will suffer.

10am

Great! I just powered through 4 hours of important work and most people have barely started.

I feel great. I feel productive. The rest of my day is going to be a breeze. I can reward myself now.

I'll take a shower, get something to eat, watch some YouTube, go see what the rest of my family are up to.

I'll take an hour off, maybe even two. Remember, I've done all the important things for the day. The rest is activities that are important but don't have to be done.

12am

It's midday and I'm ready to start my second shift. This shift is only 2 hours. It's a bit more relaxed but work still needs to get done.

These two hours are all about working on something I enjoy. It could be a new idea I've been itching to implement or a book I'd like to finish reading.

They're a fun Two hours and is a bit like a reward to my 4 hours of working on tasks I don't enjoy as much.

2pm

Now I'm completely done with work! I've achieved 4-6 hours of uninterrupted, solid work. It might not seem like a lot but it's a lot more than what most people do in their full-time desk jobs.

People waste hours chit-chatting, taking breaks, browsing the web, most doing 2-3 hours of actual work, if that!

I've achieved more than the average person and now it's time to relax and focus on other parts of my life. I mean, what's the point of all this if all I'm doing is working? You have to enjoy life or at some point, you'll get burnt out.

I'll take a nap now, get something to eat and prepare meals for the next day. I've got the next 2-3 hours to do whatever I want. I can be lazy If I want to, I deserve it.

6pm

It's time for boxing. I love boxing and have been doing it for almost a year now. At the start it was a pain but now I'm ok and can spar guys without getting beat up.

Now, I enjoy it and it's a healthy balance to sitting on my but all day.

To box, you need to be fit. Most pro boxers are semi professional runners. It's common for me to run 5-7 kms a few days a week to maintain my fitness.

I used to do no exercise before. I'd go gym here and there but that's a different type of exercise.

As a result, I was putting on unnecessary weight, getting sick and generally an a very unhealthy path.

I'll box for about an hour or two. Boxing consists of bag work, sparring, running, strength an conditioning, etc.

8pm

I've achieved my work goals, my exercise and fitness goals and my healthy eating goals, now I can relax some more before bed.

I'll watch more YouTube and maybe even a TV series I'm interested in. While doing so, I'll be writing down notes and ideas to implement the next day or the next week, basically keep my mind ticking.

10pm

It's time to sleep and so I'll get make sure everything is prepared for the next day and go to bed.

I believe it's important to get at least 7-8 hours of healthy sleep. I used to not care about this and feel sluggish most of the day. It definitely took a toll and the sluggishness would never go away.

Not, I eat healthy, drink water, sleep well and prioritise taking care of my body. A healthy body and mind will allow you to work better. Remember, it's all a balance. You can't work 10 hours a day, each day or you'll burn out and give yourself health problems, sometimes permanent.

We do this to be able to live the way we want but health is too much of a sacrifice.

The above is a routine of how my day looks like. It took me a long time to build it into a routine. I've experimented with a tonne of different things. From two hours of sleep a day, (polyphasic sleep), to working at night, and I've eventually found what works best with me.

Some people are night people while I'm a morning person. I used to be a night person but the mornings have just given me a better output when the comparison was made.

The Successful Entrepreneur

The successful Entrepreneur has a healthy balance between Work, Health and Relationships.

Sometimes you achieve more by working less. I know that sounds counterintuitive but there are many people who deceive themselves by sitting behind a laptop or computer doing activities that contribute little to success.

They'll sit there a whole 10 hours but will be distracted every 10 minutes by FaceBook or an email.

It's better to work 4 solid, uninterrupted hours than it is to sit there the whole day. You can do a lot of work in one hour if you put your mind to it.

The problem is, it takes a lot of brain power to be 100% focussed for 4 gruelling hours. For your brain to have this sort of focus you need to reward it and be in a healthy state of mind and body.

For this reason many entrepreneurs have an active fitness regime. Whether it's regular jogs in the morning or competing in a sport, sometimes even professionally, the balance is imperative to success.

This section is going to cover a few characteristics that are necessary to be successful at entrepreneurship. They're fundamentals that you either have OR have to grow into. Without them, you're leaving it to luck.

Saving Money

Not many people I know are good money savers.
In fact, I live in Australia and many people here
live paycheck to paycheck. Not that they don't
earn enough, it's more related to the fact that their
highly socially expensive life style of partying on
the weekends leaves them desperate for their next
pay.

Don't get me wrong, I love spending money. I'll
go on shopping sprees every now and then. I have
a 2015 Subaru WRX and have gone on over 6
holidays in the last 2 years BUT this has all come
out of my spending budget.

I have a savings budget that either gets invested
into stock or stored into accounts that are there for
back up purposes.

The more money you have available, the more
opportunities you can capitalise and participate in.
How many times have you seen something you
want to flip or invest in but just haven't had the
money to do it?

Commit to never being in that position again. I
know someone who would have made himself a
lot of money by now if he could only learn to
save. He depends on others investing in flipping
things although he has all the knowledge to do it

himself. He shares the profits but then spends it on something silly and he's back to square one.

The more you save, the more you can invest and the richer you'll get. It's a simple part of the money making process many people tend to overlook!

At the peak of my earnings I was selling almost shirts a day profiting $3-7k per day! It lasted around 3 weeks BUT I was pumping $5k in FaceBook advertising to be able to get that. If I didn't have money saved in the bank to be able to support that payment output then I wouldn't have made anything.

If you don't have money when the right opportunity stares you in the face and says "BUY ME!", then your going to lose out, big time.

Jot down your finances and commit to save a set dollar amount every month, spend the rest on whatever you want.

Eating Healthy

I once conducted an epic experiment on myself.

I'm a naturally skinny guy. I used to find it quite difficult to put on any weight even though I was eating like a maniac.

A friend of mine is on the other side of the scale. He's not obese but he had some weight on him he wanted to lose so he suggested this diet idea that he had read about on the internet.

It's called the raw vegan diet. You may have heard of it, you may have not. I hadn't at the time and I was all about trying new things so I joined him.

For Three weeks straight we ate nothing but raw fruits, veggies, seeds and nuts. I didn't plan my macros, (protein, carb, fat intake), I just ate whatever was fruity and fresh. This doesn't include fruit juice from the shop.

We bought a juicer and a blender and lived off salads, juices, smoothies and nuts.

The first two weeks was difficult. Real difficult. Going from eating meat regularly to stop is tough. Family members would cook up a feast and I'd have to fight through all the enticing aromas and make my juice and smoothies.

The third week is where the magic happened. I felt like a million bucks. I'd be jumping out of work at 5am ready to work. My mind was focussed on what needed to be done. I had a sudden urge to run outside and enjoy the sun. I have no idea how all these connections were being made within me but every part of me physically, emotioanly, spiritually improved 10 times. It was as if I had unlocked a secret way of living life. One full of energy. I felt I was on energy drinks and just couldn't stop smiling and generally being happy.

I'd walk into the supermarket and realise how much of the food was junk. All this crap we're putting inside us that's making us sad, groggy, sleepy, depressed, sick and everything else negative.

It was as if I had been living dead my whole life. There was no comparison between the two foods.

It was after this experience I changed everything. I went back to eating regular food but 50% of my diet consisted of good, organic fruits and veggies.

I'm able to keep up with my strict work and sports schedule only because of this. The more fruits and veggies I incorporate the better I feel.

The only way I could describe that experience

was it felt like being superhuman. I'm not exaggerating. It really felt that good.

Eating healthy is one of the most important things for me now. I might have to dedicate 1-2 hours a day of meal prep time but the work and health benefits are worth it. It _needs_ to be done and I can never go back to eating what I used to.

I know the majority of you scoff at the thought of eating healthy but you never know what your missing out on until you try. If your game enough, research the raw food diet and try it for a month. You have nothing to lose and everything to gain.

Getting Things Done

There have been ample times in my life that I've had a sudden rush of motivation followed by the feeling of wanting to quit.

I'll go a week straight of working my butt off on an idea I'm highly passionate about but then it will start to go away and I'll be left feeling like I want to do something else.

This cycle continued for a good 6 months till I realised I wasn't getting anywhere.

Since then, I've applied the 'get it done' policy. No matter how much I drop in motivation the idea is to keep moving forward until you've implemented the full idea.

If I have an idea, I'll do enough to at least test or validate it before I give up.

I wanted to try kindle publishing so I've decided to write at least 20 books before I make my decision on whether I want to continue or change my business.

Have a goal for yourself and make it achievable. Only you know yourself so only you know what these goals are.

Make them small but follow through with them. At least you'll get into the habit of competing things which is more important then working 10 hour days only to give up. It's better to work 2 hours consistently till you finish.

I learnt it the hard way. Hopfully, you'll learn from my experience.

Focus Level – Insane

I once became obsessed with Shark Tank. Me and my friends watched almost every episode for a month straight. The characters were awesome and we fell in love with the way the entrepreneurs would think.

There was a general trend to how they'd react to certain personalities.

A great characteristic to compare were the entrepreneurs who were focussed compared to the ones that weren't.

Focus means to be able to channel all your energy into the one goal until you reach it. You're not distracted by the other 10 goals in your head running around wanting a piece of your attention. You're able to put them all on the back burner until you achieve what you want.

Some entrepreneurs would come in with a great idea but would have 10-15 variations of the idea they want to launch. The Sharks/Entrepreneurs faces would drop in disappointment knowing that they can still make so much money before even thinking of expanding.

Sometimes less options are better. The less you can get people to think, the more decisive they're going to be, generally speaking.

If I come across a T-shirt idea that's selling really well, it's better to focus on maximising the sales of that design before making variations of it. When's somethings hot, you ride it till it's not hot anymore.

This is focus, being able to push junk out of your head and to reach your goal(s), everytime.

I'll give you another example.

My first full-time job was at a Civil Engineering firm. I was the assistant junior engineer who'd help the senior guys with their projects. We build pipelines for contractors and the government. Some projects were small, some were quite large, either way, I'd have a tonne of tasks to do everyday.

I'd have a list of things to do and would work on any one of them at any given time. I'd switch in between when I got bored of one task and switch back to it when I got bored of the other.

My manager on the other hand would also have a list _except_, instead of doing what I did. He'd order them in terms of which were the most critical tasks and work through the list strictly throughout this order till he finished. He'd only move on to the next task once the previous was done 100%.

At the end of the day, I would have finished 2-3 things whereas, he would have finished 10.

It was astonishing how much of a difference it made. He'd close all unrelated work tabs until this task was done.

This is what I implement now. I work on one task until it's 100% done. Then, I'll work on the next. My productivity has been able to improve astronomically.

Long Term Play

Business is a long term play. Longer term than most people think. Too many ebooks, courses and gumtree ads make it feel like getting rich is just around the corner.

It might have been for some people but for most, it takes some time to start learning the ropes and making money. Once you realise this, you're ready to give it the necessary time and consistency that it needs.

I work on projects for weeks, months even when i'm not making a single dollar for them. But I know my success ratio is around 10% which means 1 out of 10 things I try will generally work!

All I have to do now is to try 10 things as quickly as possible and i'll continue to have those successes which cover for my fails and add more money into my bank account.

When I started designing shirts for my previous business, it took me 50 designs to see a single sale.

The next 50-200 designs bought in almost 300k in revenue.

Most people would have quit at 5 designs. It was

exhausting researching, designing, setting up FaceBook advertising and repeating the process time and time again with no luck but I knew others were making money so it was just a matter of time till I figured it out myself!

Final Words

Entrepreneurship is a long and windy road. With it's fair share of ups and downs.

Some people can handle it, some people can't. Once you've tasted that feeling of success however, it will stay with you forever and will have you addicted to the chase.

You don't have to get everything right straight off the bat. In fact, no one does. You learn by implementation and making mistakes. Only your mistakes will point out what you need to work on.

Learn to be comfortable with failing. With things not working out how you planned. Adapting is more important than anything in this industry and everyday will bring it's own set of challenges.

Some entrepreneurs describe even successful business ventures as feeling as though everything would crash at any given moment.

On the bright side, business is an escape. It's an escape into a reality you create for yourself. You have ultimate control in how much money you're happy with, how much time you want to spend on your business, when you want to work, when you want to take breaks, when you want to spend time with friends and everything in between.

Not many people can enjoy the luxuries the business lifestyle brings with it. I definitely encourage everyone to give it a shot. At the very least, you'll learn a lot and might be able to return to business sometime later at a whole new level. Whatever you decide to do, I wish you the best of luck and know you'll get there easily as long as you keep moving forward!

- Mateen S

Join Over 1,000 People in our Insider List

Insiders get Business Case Studies, Income Reports, the below upcoming Book Titles for free upon launch and much much more!

Join Here ^ *http://goo.gl/jQn9ou*
COMING SOON

Author Bio

Mateen has loved entrepreneurship since school. Buying and selling USB's, phones and game consoles on eBay and Gumtree, he learned the art of the hustle young.

Two years into his engineering career he quit to dedicate himself to entrepreneurship and take it to the next level.

Three years since the day he's quit from work life, he's made six figures from a variety of different entrepreneurship avenues. From selling merchandise on the famous Teespring platform to blogging. He's blog, affengineer.com, has been featured on prominent websites and is known to be the best for Teespring information.

He dedicates himself to finding ways to make money and sharing it with his insider list to create a community comfortable with sharing information and helping each other get to the financial place they desire.